The Souled-Out

CHURCH

Is the Church Damaged Goods?

Kevin Gibbs

Scripture references are from the NIV and KJV
Limits of Liability and Disclaimer of Warranty
This is a work of creative nonfiction. The events are portrayed to the best of the author's memory. While all the stories in this book are true, some names and identifying details have been changed to protect the privacy of the people involved.

The purpose of this book is to educate and entertain. The author and/or publisher do not guarantee that anyone following these techniques, suggestions, tips, ideas, or strategies will become successful. The author and/or publisher shall have neither liability nor responsibility to anyone with respect to any loss or damage caused, or alleged to be caused, directly or indirectly by the information contained in this book.

Editor: Shavonna Bush

Interior Designer: Laura Brown

ISBN: 978-1-7368982-0-8

Bush Legacy Publishing
Chattanooga, TN 37421

Contents

Acknowledgments

I dedicate this book to my late father, Cerdan Collins, who died on August 2, 2019. He and I had a rocky relationship for much of my adult life, but by the grace of God, we were able to overcome and grew close, for which I am so incredibly grateful. While spending time together during Thanksgiving of 2018, he read parts of the manuscript from my first book, *Will Somebody Please Listen*, and was excited about the material. You could see how proud he was that I was taking on writing, and he was truly looking forward to the day I would officially become a published author. I wish you were here to see that I made it pops–RIH.

To other members of my family (mother, stepfather, stepmother, children, grandchildren, siblings, and wife), I love each of you more than words can describe. From the depth of my heart, I thank you for all the support shown to me and all the words of encouragement you have given about my writing. In some form or fashion, all of you have been pillars for me throughout this process or whatever it is I have set out to achieve.

I also thank my church family, Zion Missionary Baptist of Jackson, Georgia, for the continued support they have given unto Shae and me as their Senior Pastor and 1st Lady–and for being an integral part of our lives. You have provided us with many great memories, and prayerfully, there are many more to come.

Lastly, I want to give a special thanks to my publisher, Shavonna Bush (Bush Legacy Publishing), for inspiring me to write this second book and for the help she has provided whenever I needed to call on her. I commend both her and her husband, Dorian, for stepping out on faith to start their own publishing company and for taking on my wife and me as their first clients. Blessings to you guys!

While I have called out specific names of some family and friends, let it be clearly understood: I am grateful unto all who have shown their support by purchasing my material, reading it, sharing it, or whatever means of support you have provided. You are no less important! In fact, without you, there is no me–for if I have no supporters or readers, I certainly have no reason to write.

Preface

If you are reading these words, then it is necessary that I give you a great big "thanks" for allowing me to have your attention. I am not a betting man, but if I were, I would bet on the probability you were drawn to the title or cover of the book. I am guessing that it piqued your interest just enough to want to find out what type of information lies within the pages. Should that be the reason you are currently holding this book in your hands, then kudos to my publisher for convincing me how important a cover is (something I did not give much thought to when writing my first book). It was made perfectly clear to me that the old adage, "don't judge a book by its cover," is not exactly true anymore, as today's reader is drawn first to the outward appearance and a catchy title. With that said, I guess you can teach an old dog a new trick after all!

It is important to note that the topics set forth in this writing are generated from personal experience, conversations with fellow ministry leaders, and observing people's behavior in the religious arena. While they form the basis of my arguments, I do not attempt to come across as having superior knowledge on any of the subjects presented; instead, I simply offer my viewpoint and opinion. After having served twenty-four years in the ministry (eighteen as pastor), I have begun to clearly see why so many people are turned off by religion-specifically when it comes to the Christian church.

It seems the desire for many to attend church has diminished through the years, and I attribute the primary reason is they're tired of all the shenanigans. The church is supposed to be like a hospital where people come for spiritual healing. It is supposed to be a gathering of genuine people who are believers in God and His divine word; and a place where the atmosphere is filled with love, unity, mercy, compassion, and forgiveness. Church is supposed to be a pillar in our communities and a place to turn to, especially during crisis moments (whether socially, economically, or psychologically).

Instead, what we see from the church today is quite disturbing. It is enough to make some question its legitimacy, and that is ever so unfortunate. In a sense, the church has become a laughingstock; it is the brunt of many jokes, and some people's mindset seems to be-why be bothered with a phony group of worshipers? What is the purpose of attending church if what I find there is equal to what I am dealing with in the world? While I am not proud to say this: "Who can blame them for such thinking?"

Now, I expect that some will disagree with my viewpoints. You may feel I have lost sight of the fact that no pastor or congregation is perfect (or as we so often say, the church is made up of imperfect people); therefore, there are bound to be problems. Believe me – that is not the case at all. I totally understand and do keep those things into consideration as I write. Perhaps you may even question my theological perspective. However, before you do, I wish to remind you that no individual has cornered the market on theology. The fact is, the theological perspective of every person can be questioned in some fashion or another. If yours happens to be a little more profound than mine or a little more astute, then praise be to God, but please don't tune me out as a result.

My prayer is that you read this information objectively. Do not let your personal feelings or opinions of me (or what you think you know of me) influence your judgment. One thing I am sure you will not be able to disagree with– is that the church has an image problem. Of course, it is not the entire church, just factions, but nonetheless, there is a dilemma! And now that I have your attention, let us reason together as we consider where or with whom lies the problem.

Introduction

Allow me to begin by first addressing the title. Many of you are no doubt familiar with the term "sell-out," which – among the urban culture – is often used in a disparaging manner. It is suggestive of someone having betrayed something to which they are said to owe allegiance. The term is particularly offensive to the African American community because it refers to blacks who knowingly or with gross negligence act against the interest of blacks as a whole.

The title of this book is derived from that term, but with a slight play on words as I use the word "souled" as opposed to "sold." Some may feel it is a bit misleading because of the impression it gives. On the surface, it sounds like an indictment upon the entire church body; It carries the notion the church has compromised its integrity, morality, authenticity, and principles in exchange for personal gain. But the truth is, the whole of the church is simply fine. We are made certain of that by virtue of what Christ says to Peter in the "B" part of Matthew 16:18,

> *"...and upon this rock I will build my church; and the gates of hell shall not prevail against it." (KJV).*

Contrary to the popular belief of students of scripture, sometimes common sense must factor into our understanding of biblical texts. You see, Jesus is the master builder, and he has emphatically declared the gates of hell will not triumph over that which he builds. In essence, Satan's kingdom has no pathway to victory over the kingdom Christ constructs. If such is the case, and yet we can clearly see some churches today have questionable character(s)–how does that get explained? Easy! The term *church* has a dual meaning. On the one hand, it refers to the universal church body, while on the other hand, it is referencing the local church body (which reflects the universal body). What Jesus speaks of in Matthew 16:18 is the universal body or the collective body of believers across the globe.

When I speak of the *souled-out church*, I am specifically referring to factions of the universal body, which are the local churches. It is there, where in many cases, it can be said the church has compromised its integrity, morality, authenticity, and principles in exchange for personal gain.

Unfortunately, some are causing the image of the universal body to be smeared, or at the very least, they are casting doubt about the credibility of the whole church! However, as I go back to what Jesus declares in Matthew 16:18, I think it is imperative to consider a key-word-*prevail*. That word means to overcome, and Jesus is simply stating that Satan's kingdom shall not overcome the church he builds. He is not suggesting that Satan will not be able to inflict harm upon the church, which is precisely what he's doing through the auspices of some local churches. So, in that sense, the church or

15

factions of it has lost its soul, which is the focal point of my message, thus providing the motive to come up with the term *souled-out*.

When we think of the word soul, we think of the spiritual or immaterial part of a human being or animal regarded as immortal. In some cases, it could reference the emotional and intellectual energy or intensity of someone or something. I want to look at it from the spiritual or immaterial aspect of the human being who is the church by all accounts in the Bible. It must be noted that the building (or structure) in which many of us gather with others for worship – is not the actual church. The Greek word *ekklesia* means called-out assembly. In general, it refers to all people who follow Christ without respect to locality or time. Regardless of who they are or where they gather, such a group should be spiritual above anything else. Jesus declares in John 4:24,

"God is a Spirit: and they that worship Him must worship Him in spirit and in truth." (KJV).

Unfortunately, however, not all are, and therefore

I want to shed light on the damaging role of some people that you may very well find yourself in fellowship with. Yet, for the sake of encouragement, I must go back to Matthew 16:18 once more and remind you that Jesus said, the gates of hell shall not overcome his church. While what we are witnessing in the house of God today is discouraging, there is a reason for hope to remain in the heart of those who are genuine believers. Needless-to-say, there is also work for us to do. In Psalm 94:16, a question is asked that every true child of God must consider and answer:

> *"Who will rise up for me against the*
> *evildoers? Or who will stand up for me*
> *against the workers of iniquity?" (KJV).*

My answer is an emphatic "Me!" Through this writing, I will do my best to expose Satan's works that I see are prevalent throughout the membership of local churches. My prayer is that you will be enlightened by what I say and that you will join me in standing up against the enemy's work!

The Devil in the Pulpit

Perhaps the primary reason many local churches appear to be souled-out starts with looking at who occupies the pulpit. No sincere person wants to imagine that the men or women who stand to preach the gospel are anything more than called servants of God. The sad fact of the matter is that is not the case. Some are called while others are not. Of those who are not called servants, an alarming number of them are atheists; they do not actually believe a word of the Bible in which they preach.

I will never forget the first time I heard this. While attending online courses at a seminary in Kentucky, I would often read the weekly address from the school's president, who was a prominent historical theologian within the Baptist denomination. One address stood out to me particularly, as he brought attention to the many unbelieving preachers who occupy pulpits in churches across the nation. The story was intriguing enough that I did further research and discovered that a significant number of pastors simply view what they do as an occupation. Some suggested they lost their belief while going through seminary. Others are on record, admitting they were drawn to ministry because they were enamored with the glamor, prestige, and notoriety which is often associated with the position in today's world.

I was dumbfounded! It is perplexing to think of men (and some women) having the audacity to stand before congregations of people and pretend to be delivering a message from God, when in fact, God is far from their minds. What is even more disconcerting is the fact that some of them are extremely convincing. They have an in-depth knowledge of scripture and an astute ability to appear as though they are under the anointing of the Holy

Spirit, but the reality of the matter is many are just con artists. I know this firsthand because I fell victim to it.

In 2011, while attending a prominent Bible College in Atlanta, Georgia–I met a local pastor in the area who was also there taking classes to obtain certification. This brother was an established senior pastor of a well-known church in East Atlanta and had achieved much academically already–or so I assumed because of having the title Dr. before his name. To be honest, I was a bit surprised he was taking basic level classes for certification. Nevertheless, I have learned not everything is meant for me to understand. Almost immediately, we connected and became friends. Not long afterwards, he began inviting me to his church, but because my wife was loyal to her home church, I was reluctant to ask her to join me. Therefore, I kept telling him I'll show up one day.

The opportunity presented itself when he asked me to come and be the guest preacher one Sunday. My wife was always anxious to hear me preach, and I knew she would not hesitate to support me, so I accepted the invitation. We went, and she had the chance to meet this brother, and to my surprise, she suggested we go back soon so we could hear him preach (He had a natural ability to charm people).

Our visit back to listen to him was all it took. His gift wowed me. I happen to love good preaching and teaching, and as they say in some church circles – he could bring it! Eventually, I chose to connect with his ministry because I strongly felt that is where I needed to be. You see, at the time, I was also at a crossroads in my life; I had sort of lost focus and lost my way. I was in the midst of a transition from Kentucky to Georgia, and let's just say, I was not making very wise decisions. Some old inner demons had reared their ugly heads, and I was letting them get the best of me. So, I became convinced God was speaking to me through whom I presumed to be His servant.

Unfortunately, what I would soon discover led to quite the disappointment! In short, the brother was a shyster; he was being deceptive to the congregation and was trying to recruit me to join with his shenanigans. Before I go any further, I must say that I still believe God used him to get my attention. Biblical accounts show God can use whatever or whoever He desires to get His message across. One of my favorite passages in the Old Testament is found in Numbers (22nd chapter), when God spoke through the mouth of a donkey to the soothsayer, Balaam. If God can open the mouth of a donkey and speak through it, then most certainly, He can open the mouth of any man (servant or not) and get His message to whoever. Regardless of how things would turn out, I received what God desired for me to have!

Back to the situation, thankfully, it did not take long for me to see what was happening, and therefore, my wife and I left almost as quickly as we came. Here is the thing, though – I left in body, yet my mind stayed behind because I could not stop thinking of those who were blind to what was going on. At this point, I began to look at the church with a whole new perspective! It is one thing to hear about stuff like this and another to witness it firsthand.

Many congregations are captivated by their pastor,

and little do they realize they're being captivated by Satan himself (or his disciple). Seduction is a real threat to God's people. Satan's number one goal is to corrupt the mind of believers and lead them away from the simplicity that is in Christ Jesus. In other words, he wants to lead them away from devotion, loyalty, and commitment to Christ. The best way for this to occur is for Satan to disguise himself as a righteous servant of God (a.k.a. preacher). One of the Apostle Paul's main objectives was to expose the false teachers that had infiltrated the church in what we know as the 2nd letter to the Corinthians. He made it quite clear that men were masquerading as apostles of Christ, and this should not be a surprise because:

"Satan himself masquerades as an angel
of light." (II Corinthians 11:14...NIV).

Let's go back to the point about common sense again and consider the following question(s): Why would Satan do anything else but parade around the church as an angel of light? Why would he expose himself and make it easy for people to recognize who he is? In warfare, the enemy looks for every advantage he can gain over his opponent, and I can assure you that exposing himself is not one of them. Don't you think he knows if we can easily discern who he is that we will better prepare ourselves against his schemes? Satan has been called many names (i.e., serpent, devil, snake, deceptive, demonic), but the one thing no person can call him is *dumb*. The Bible says in Genesis 3:1,

> *"Now the serpent was more crafty than*
> *any of the wild animals the Lord God had*
> *made." (NIV).*

Having said that, let's contemplate how he poses as a servant of righteousness. Naturally, he stresses the life and teachings of Jesus; he highlights all the good qualities of life and all the traits that characterize people. He even tells people to copy the life of Jesus and focus their hearts upon these good qualities of life, and if they do, God will accept them. But he makes one fatal mistake; he does not follow his own instructions. He does not completely embody the true character of Christ. Never has that been so obvious to me as it has in the past few years.

It started with what I saw from the brother I had momentarily been duped into becoming friends with while attending Bible College. Once again, this man was a great orator, a fantastic teacher, educated in the word, and dynamic in his delivery. I could go on and on with the accolades. I have always been proud of having a spirit of discernment; usually, I'm pretty good at recognizing the caliber of person someone is – but I didn't see this one! (Even the best of people gets had sometimes).

It wasn't until after I witnessed some things behind the scenes that I saw a person who did not embody the true character of Christ, not even in the slightest. The church was a hustle for him; it was all about the money, and I believe he felt I was gullible enough to fall for his tricks. Something about the way we interacted on the college campus must have convinced him I was like-minded and would be a good recruit. If so, I am baffled as to how he came to such a conclusion. Nevertheless, I am delighted to be able to say that is not my character. Of course, I do not mean to imply I have no flaws because that would be untruthful. I am a person of many short-comings (To be discussed in a later chapter). However, I do not believe anyone who knows me can honestly question my character or see me as a shyster; at least, I hope not.

Of course, I understand that all depends on what your perception of character is. I feel there is a difference in having flawed behavior versus having an outright egregious disposition. We all have defects in our nature, but not everyone is appalling in their behavior – such as making choices motivated by pure greed, narcissism, hate, etc. Life's experience has shown me, people like this will intentionally hurt anyone who gets in their way to get what they desire. I speak with confidence as I tell you; such a label does not apply to me!

I have nothing but the utmost respect for the church, including when I was in the world doing my thing (before ministry). It has always been, in my eyes, a sacred place and a symbol of protection. If at no other time, people ought to be able to come into the Lord's house and feel they have entered a safe haven, a place of refuge where they do not have to be subjected to the same issues that occur every day in life outside the church walls. People ought to feel love, unity, and peace as they engulf themselves in the worship experience.

I find it appalling when people deliberately do hurtful things to destroy all of that. I think it is disgusting to see how preaching is looked upon as a money-making opportunity instead of a sacred and privileged assignment. It is horrific for someone to stand up in the pulpit and play with God's word, including those who like to entertain. It is sickening to proclaim yourself as a believer and yet do not make any concerted effort to live like one because, in reality, you are an atheist. What we are witnessing from some preachers today is enough to make those who are putting forth every effort to be genuine have a desire to quit. Sometimes that thought crosses my mind, but then I keep plugging along, all while being reminded of something Paul says in I Corinthian 9:16:

> *"For though I preach the gospel, I have*
> *nothing to glory of: for necessity is laid*
> *upon me; yea, woe is unto me, if I preach*

not the gospel!" (KJV).

Two things jump out at me when I read that verse; first, the *necessity* laid upon Paul. All preachers who are genuinely called can relate to those words, as the feeling is one of being compelled to communicate the word of God. The second is the declaration of *woe*. Paul suggests that if he doesn't do what is required of him in preaching the gospel, there will be a steep price to pay for *woe* carries the notion of misery or disaster. Whenever I feel like I want to quit, I am reminded of the requirement, by virtue of the calling, and the consequences I would suffer if I failed to keep preaching the gospel.

Now, let us consider a question: what is the gospel? First and foremost, it is the joyous good news of salvation in Jesus the Christ. You can say it is the fulfillment of God's plan of salvation, which began in Israel, completed in Jesus, and is made known by the church. You may have heard it referred to as the *gospel of the grace of God* or the *gospel of the glory of Christ,* but that is not to imply there is more than one gospel. The former emphasizes the good news originates in God and His grace, while the latter simply emphasizes the good news comes to man through the person of Jesus – for he is the gospel. God's good news was present in the life, teaching, and atoning death of Jesus. Being that is the case, let us briefly focus on how he lived and what he taught because every true believer's primary responsibility is to mimic His life in every way.

Any person who dares to call themselves a preacher and has read and studied the Bible yet fails to acknowledge that the way of righteousness is a mandate upon their life – would have to be a complete idiot. If such a person cannot see that living the gospel is as important as preaching it, they truly have no business standing in the pulpit. Likewise, if they refuse to accept that Jesus advocated for justice and mercy to be shown to all people, had compassion for the poor, under-privileged, mistreated people of the world, and loved every man, woman, boy, or girl irrespective of religion, creed, or color – then he or she has a blatant disregard for the authentic gospel message. Should they keep silent against acts of injustice, hatred, and bigotry-or should they even support someone who exemplifies these things – they are nothing more than a fraud! As it stands, we are witnessing an enormous amount of fraudulent preaching in many local churches.

I'll even go a step further and make the case that much of this is spearheaded by white conservative evangelical pastors. Now, before you determine you've had enough and decide to close the book, please hear the rationale behind such a bold statement. Prayerfully, by adding some context, you will see why I dare say what I say. Remember, I mentioned that the one fatal mistake made by Satan and his disciples is they do not embody the very things some boldly preach as angels of light. Publicly, they stand up and say all the right stuff and give the impression they have concern for others. They pretend to be on the side of righteousness, justice, equality, and unity. They love to emphasize what morals and Christian values they have. Yet, what they say, and what they do is altogether different.

Right now, it is November 21, 2020. I provide this information to reference the time of this writing because it is very significant to what I'm about to say. At this moment, America is under the leadership of one of the worst individuals to ever hold the office of President of the United States. He is *arrogant, narcissistic, hateful, divisive*, a *bully*, a *racist,* and full of *evil*. Perhaps it sounds a bit brash to describe another person in this manner, yet I stand by what I say, and the reason I have no qualms about it is because he possesses all the character traits that God despises. Do not let that be confused with God hating the person – for that is simply not true. He only hates the character of the person or any individual who possesses such a personality. So as children of God, it is well within our right to feel the same way while also exposing these types of people (Don't forget about the question in Psalm 94:16).

His official reign began at noon on January 20, 2017, following one of the most shocking surprises in election history (November 2016). Not many were expecting him to become President, especially after he had given us a preview of his character during both the primary and presidential debates–not to mention his antics during campaign tours. As a respected colleague of mine likes to say: "When a person shows you who they are, believe them." This man showed us exactly who he was, and if no one else believed it, I certainly did.

As it turned out, not everyone felt as I did because it didn't prevent the majority of voters from choosing to elect him anyway. Upon his first day in office, he validated his skeptics' concerns and left no doubt the nation was in trouble. I'm not going to spend time talking about all of his misdeeds because such needs to be written in a book all by themselves, and besides, it will take away from the point I'm trying to drive home. What needs to be understood is that some of his biggest supporters were white conservative evangelical pastors, men, and women who stand preaching a gospel message but support the works of Satan. Many of them are on record stating that this president, with all his wickedness, is a righteous servant of God. Imagine that!

If you are a student of the Bible, think about how that stands in contradiction to the idea of righteousness according to scripture. What more can be said, except that it is the action of fraudulent people, and it is deeply hurting the church's image. If you are under the leadership of such a person, the question is – what's your move? Are you willing to stand up for the true righteousness of God, or will you simply turn the other way?

Wishy-Washy Church Members

In this chapter, I want to focus specifically upon the pew sitters, some of whom I will label as *Wishy-Washy Church Members*. Maybe it is better to classify them as sometimes people; sometimes they act like real Christians, and sometimes they do not. For my argument, I will stay with the former. Besides, I like the sound of it better.

It is easy to pin the troubles of the local church upon the pastor since he or she stands as the leader. In every arena of life, sports, business, religion, family, work, etc., everything pretty much begins and ends with the person who is seen as the head. But to be fair, all problems are not their fault! I often use an axiom that says: *"You can lead a horse to the water, but you cannot make him drink it."* How fitting that is for the pastor and congregation of any church. No group of people assembled for religious worship, which may be dealing with an image crisis or character issues, can lay all the blame at the pastor's feet because members play a role also – or in some cases, more so.

Again, it is disconcerting to know that many pulpits are occupied with men and women who do not believe a word in the Bible; therefore, they do not adhere to its teaching. It is equally disturbing to know that the pews are filled with the same type of people. Some may argue there is a difference. Whereas the pulpit is typically filled with learned individuals, the pews are occupied by many who are unlearned. Perhaps that is true, yet it is no less excusable. It only makes matters worse!

No man or woman should be sitting in church unlearned, except maybe the one who is a new convert. But even then, it is inexcusable to remain in such a state because if you are there for all the right reasons, you will accept nothing less than learning and growing in the word of God. Conversion carries the idea of someone having a change of attitude that brings them into a right relationship with God; it involves turning away from evil deeds and false worship while turning toward serving and worshiping the Lord. Some may disagree, but I happen to believe included in the conversion experience is also an appetite for truth, yearning to mature, and wanting to live in a manner pleasing to God. The whole idea behind sitting under the influence of preaching and teaching is so that these things may happen; that one may grow in the knowledge of the Lord – to learn the statutes, teachings, and principles of our God, to uphold them, or at least strive to uphold them!

If a converted person feels as though they are not growing, then it is the individual's responsibility to go where they genuinely believe they hear divine instruction. Jesus declares in John 10:27 *(KJV)*,

"My sheep hear my voice, and I know

them, and they follow me.''

Just a few verses prior, he declares:

"And a stranger will they not follow but
will flee from him: for they know not the
voice of stranger." (John 10:5 KJV).

Those verses alone suggest it is improbable for one to be a true convert and yet sit in church unlearned; it is only natural that the spirit within them desires to grow – and they will! They will not listen to a voice that is alien or foreign or not feeding them with the righteous word of God.

Now, this is not to say every person, who is converted, will be on the same level intellectually, for some grasp and comprehend things at a higher rate of speed than others – there is nothing wrong with that. I am not the fastest of learners myself, yet I am also not the slowest. I consider myself to be somewhere in between, and once more, it is okay because your level of intellect, neither the speed by which you learn, has any bearing on your conversion. What is important is for every converted person to simply do what they know to do while trusting God to do the rest, and if they will, then no church pew will be occupied with someone utterly oblivious to the teachings of scripture. The Bible emphasizes the need for us to study God's word (II Timothy 2:15), and if we will put forth the effort to rightly divide – or cut straight to the truth-we are certain not to be ignorant of what is right or wrong in the church.

When we genuinely invite God into our lives and allow Him to lead, guide, or direct our pathway; Jesus promised,

> *"When he, the Spirit of truth (a.k.a. the Holy Spirit), is come, he will guide you into all truth…" (John 16:13a KJV).*

This means, the moment we sincerely give ourselves to the Lord, His spirit will take up residence within us, directing our footsteps to persistently walk in the way of truth as it pertains to all things.

So then, sitting in the pew as an unlearned believer does not cut it for me in connection to this argument. I prefer to see it as the church filled with many who are wishy-washy members. The term wishy-washy implies a person is indecisive or uncertain; they waver back and forth. Indecisive church members are peculiar, not in a good way because one day they are holier-than-thou, and the next day you cannot distinguish them from the average Joe who has no affiliation with a church. I lean toward the belief that they have not been fully converted, if at all, and neither do they possess the right spirit.

Some are in the church simply because of other family members. There is no connection to God, no desire to hear the word, no willingness to change the way they live, no aspirations to carry on the legacy of Christ – they are just there because they want to be with their family or carry on the family tradition of being a member of the church. Then there are those in attendance who merely like having a religious association because it looks good on the resume. These are the people who are more prone to look away from the truth, the righteous way of doing things, or they look the other way when their supposed leader is doing underhanded stuff because just maybe they have some stake in their unscrupulous deeds as well. That, to me, is just as bad as having fraudulent preachers in the pulpit, and together, they create an ugly stain upon the church's image.

Let me bring to your remembrance something Jesus said during his infamous sermon on the mount:

"For I tell you that unless your
righteousness surpasses that of the
Pharisees and the teachers of the law, you
will certainly not enter the kingdom of
heaven." (Matthew 5:20 NIV).

What precipitated this remark? First, it is necessary to identify the meaning of the word righteousness as used in that passage. Jesus was referring to integrity, virtue, purity of life, correct thinking, feeling, and behavior. In the Pharisee's case, they lacked these things; they had a form of righteousness (or an outward appearance of such), but inwardly, many were full of corruption. It was only when it seemed to benefit them in some capacity that interest to act righteously surfaced. Otherwise, they were your classic wishy-washy church members and leaders. For evidence, I present to you John 8:1-11, where lies the story of the woman taken in adultery.

The teachers of the law and Pharisees had brought before Jesus a woman they caught in the act of adultery to see how he would rule on the situation. Their only motive was to trap him, to see if they could get him to contradict the Law of Moses. The reason was birthed out of increased anger with Jesus as he had repeatedly confronted and exposed them. Attempts to arrest him or get the people to stop believing in him were unsuccessful, so they trapped him with a situation in which there was no right answer, or so it was thought. They desperately sought a way to accuse him of being illegitimate in his claims to be the Son of God. In their minds, this was the perfect opportunity!

According to the Law of Moses, the punishment called for stoning all parties involved because their actions attack the very heart of family and society. Yet, because adultery had become so common during this time, the law was often ignored. Many people disagreed with the punishment, and even Roman authorities banned capital punishment from the Jews. Nonetheless, some prominent Jewish leaders were trying to set Jesus up, anyway. The funny thing is, they only brought accusations against the woman and not the man. This was a true disregard for the authentic Law of Moses. As they pressed the issue and continued to question Jesus about the matter, finally, he stood up and declared:

> *"If any one of you is without sin, let him be*
> *the first to throw a stone at her."*
>
> *(John 8:7 NIV).*

Can you imagine what must have been a surprising response of–Whoa-Whoa! There was no way they could do that because it would expose them even further. These religious leaders were committing an act of sin by looking the other way when it came to the man. If nothing else, their action was a display of sexism or prejudice, which is something God frowns upon. More than likely, it was something they had been teaching the people at some point or another. Jesus' response presented quite a dilemma and messed up their devious little plan!

Amazingly, this does not prevent them from trying these same methods in future endeavors; and what is even more amazing is how this epitomizes the character of people who frequently sit in the pews of the local church today. Many choose to look the other way when it comes to various sinful misdeeds committed all around them until it becomes an opportunistic moment to take advantage. They are fully aware of the transgressions taking place with their leaders – they know about the lies, the corruption, the infidelity, the stealing, etc. They know about their fellow church members' indiscretions even, but they simply look away until circumstances change, causing them to have a desire to act righteously suddenly.

Usually, when this happens, it is because someone has made them mad or something does not go their way (hence wishy-washy). That is not the mark of a true believer; instead, it has all the markings of a person who has no spirit of Christ or lacks spirituality. It is a sad indictment upon the local church body, which reflects the universal church, to have as its member's wishy-washy people.

Now, let me guess, it probably sounds to you like I have an accountability issue. Well, nothing could be further from the truth! My issue is not with accountability; my issue is with the consistency of holding one accountable. I have no problem with fellow believers holding me liable for my behavior so long as they stay consistent in doing so. Don't look the other way on any of my misdeeds and then suddenly decide to show yourself righteous by holding me accountable for something out of spite because I said something you didn't like, did something that offended you, or maybe even exposed you for something you've been doing.

Paul says to the believers at Corinth:

"Therefore, my dear brothers, stand firm.
Let nothing move you. Always give
yourselves fully to the work of the Lord..."
(I Corinthian 15:58 NIV).

In a nutshell, that is his way of telling the church to be consistent with their actions. Let us honor God by upholding the principles of His word with regularity and not when we feel like it for our convenience. The inconsistent behavior brings the authenticity of the church into question; it is the very thing that youngsters and non-believers alike bring up when talking about why they prefer to stay away from the church. The only thing is, they do not refer to it as inconsistency; instead, they call it being *fake*.

The Real Case of Hypocrisy

I have been connected to church all my life – not necessarily a faithful member, though. As a child, I grew up in the Methodist faith, but it quickly became apparent that the only time we were attending service was during special occasions. For instance, I recall how we would always go to church during Easter, a time when everybody seemed to be present. That never felt right. It appeared we were participating in a fashion event because everyone got new outfits during Easter and could not wait to wear them to church.

After I reached a certain age, I remember asking my mother if I could stop going because I wanted no part in attending to show off my new duds. To my surprise, I never received a rebuke; in fact, she stopped going too. As I think back to that moment, it just confirms, for me, that we were not in church for the right reason.

Of course, I did not completely stay away because I occasionally found my way back into a church (specifically while serving in the military). Again, it was never a serious commitment. However, in 1994, shortly after my 30th birthday, there was a sudden shift in my feelings. That was the year I got saved, and my perspective on life began to change. Something inside me was being drawn to the church, but I didn't know how to explain it to anyone; neither did I fully understand it myself. As the feeling deepened, I simply decided to go to my mother and ask if she was interested in returning with me, and she said yes. What a relief because, for some reason, going by myself was not an option. While I was thrilled by her response, there was one stipulation, I was not interested in returning to the old Methodist faith. As it turned out, neither was she.

So, it began. We started our search for a new place of worship, which ended up being a Baptist church where, ironically, I would eventually end up becoming pastor (that's a story for another time). Not long after our initial visit, we were moved to join as members and started attending each Sunday faithfully. Finally, it all felt right; I knew I was in church for good reasons! I was excited about hearing the preached word. I looked forward to being in the fellowship of other believers and embracing the atmosphere of worship. I found joy and peace being in the house of God.

Equally gratifying was seeing how my mother felt the same way and, a short time later, witnessing other family members joining us. From that moment until now (some 26 years later), church has been a way of life for my family and me. It has been incredible; it has been great; it has been awesome – and then again; it hasn't. Wait a minute! Isn't that an oxymoron? How can church be all those amazing things and not be at the same time?

Let's just say, the more I began to grow in the knowledge of God's word and understand the expectations which are upon us as believers, the more I began to see how so many were falling short in that regard. I started to see people acting one way during worship service, which was completely different from how they acted when not in church. Basically, the more I kept going to church, the more my eyes were opened to the phoniness that is prevalent among a lot of members, and at a certain point, it started becoming a challenge to deal with.

To be honest, my enthusiasm for attending church today has been somewhat zapped–but only in the sense of not being so excited to be in the fellowship of certain people. When you witness real hypocrisy among folks who call themselves children of God, or those who claim to have the Holy Spirit that is a disappointment that words cannot describe. It ignites unpleasant feelings of which I would rather avoid.

For the record, I am not suggesting that exposure to such hypocrisy came early in my walk, nor from the church my mother and I worshipped. As I grew spiritually and got involved in ministry, I would often fellowship with many other churches (white, black, etc.). I had the distinct opportunity to be a guest preacher at several rural churches in various Kentucky counties; that is no small feat when you consider many of them were all white congregations. It was nothing for me, and sometimes a few of my family members, to be the only people of color in the fellowship.

It needs to be explained that my disappointment is not in the *character* aspect of hypocrisy. Instead, it lies with the *feeling* aspect. Keep in mind, I have already stated at the beginning of this book that some may not agree with my theological perspective, and I am okay with you not doing so – but at least keep hearing me out!

Allow me to reiterate how I realize no one is perfect; we all have some shortcomings and defects in our character. With that said, I am not in any way concerned about a church member who slips up and cusses, so long as it is not a consistent part of their vocabulary. I am not concerned with a member who indulges in a little alcoholic beverage because I have grown enough to know what scripture teaches regarding such situations.

*"What goes into someone's mouth does
not defile them, but what comes out of*

51

their mouth, that is what defiles them."
(Matthew 15:11 NIV).

If anything, I am concerned whether they understand the importance of not becoming a stumbling block for others. I am not concerned with the errors made behind poor choices if there is godly sorrow and repentance for the mistakes. I am not concerned about the occasional bad attitude that creates friction among members because we all experience things that cause us not to have good days. Besides, in every family, there are going to be random squabbles. I just pray we all understand our obligation when they happen. If you have done something to offend me and realize what you have done and wish to apologize, it becomes my responsibility to accept your apology and vice-versa. The list is endless of the character traits in which I am not concerned. After all, why should I be when you consider the who's-who list of people in the Bible that had character defects:

> ➢ Adam sinned in the garden by disobeying a direct order from God.

> ➢ Abraham, the father of faith, lied not once but

twice about his wife.

➢ Moses killed an Egyptian and buried him in the sand.

➢ Samson got his haircut in the wrong barbershop (messing with Delilah).

➢ Solomon had a thousand women and still wanted more.

➢ David went after another man's wife and had her husband killed.

➢ Rahab was a prostitute.

➢ Job cursed the day he was born.

➢ Jeremiah was guilty of back-sliding.

➢ Peter denied Jesus three times out of fear and shame.

➢ Paul persecuted Christians.

Each of these people had some shortcomings, and yet all of them were great people of God who carried out the Lord's purpose in some capacity. In all the years I have been in church, I have yet to hear anyone refer to them as phonies. Therefore, if I may say again, I am not concerned with the character aspect of hypocrisy. If so, I would have to be concerned about every man, woman, boy, and girl who attends church – as each are hypocrites in that regard. There is not a person among us, who has not done something stupid, or something they regret, at some point in their life. And just because we go to church does not mean we will never do stupid things again. For the best of us cannot seem to avoid messing up!

However, what concerns me are those who never acknowledge their character defects, those who feel as if they have no flaws and therefore see no need to feel sorry for anything or work at becoming a better person. And trust me, there are people like that because I had a woman tell me directly that she had no sin in her life – for she was perfect. What is concerning is the deep-rooted feeling of hatred or disdain some have, yet they pretend to be so loving. But as scripture reminds us:

"...every tree is known by his own fruit."
(Luke 6:44 KJV).

No person can hide who they are forever; sooner or later, their real character will surface in some capacity.

What I find to be sad is how some do not know the

significance of love. John says in his first epistle:

> *"Dear friends, since God so loved us, we also ought to love one another. No one has ever seen God; but if we love one another, God lives in us and His love is made complete in us." (I John 4:11-12 NIV).*

Those words are meant for every born-again, baptized believer on the face of this planet, irrespective of race, creed, or color. But somewhere along the way, some either did not get the memo, or they ignore it because they have put limits on who they love. I like to call it selective love, which this society is noted for, and unfortunately, some churches are too.

It is no secret that America is a truly divided nation, and one of the main reasons for such division is bigotry. The so-called good ole USA is full of narrow-minded people who are intolerant of others because of their creeds, opinions, race, etc. Without question, this should not be acceptable behavior from anyone, but it is somewhat plausible when it comes from people who have no relationship with God. Therefore, I am willing to exhibit a little more patience with someone unlearned in the scripture.

Yet, when it comes to a so-called believer, I have to draw a line because no one who claims to have a love for God and a supposed understanding of His word should dare be intolerant of any other human being, except maybe for one who is living in sin. Even then, we must be careful to only show intolerance toward the sin and not the individual. No person who sits under the teaching of the holy writ and genuinely claims to embrace its principles should ever look down on someone else or have no compassion towards them, for that is the ultimate display of hypocrisy, in my opinion.

Nevertheless, that is exactly what I had a chance to see while visiting the various rural churches in my home state. They were filled with such phony people. I must confess, though; my eyes were not opened to any of this until much later in life, and a part of me is a little embarrassed by that. Then again, as they say, it is better late than never. People were sitting in the pew listening to me preach the gospel, who had no love for me at all.

Wow! It is disheartening to know these are the types of people we worship with, whether we all come together in one place or connected to the same religious faith and beliefs.

The world has witnessed more of this type of so-called Christian than it has one who is genuine, and it is no wonder the integrity or credibility of the church is being questioned. This hypocrisy was really on display during slavery, as many within the Caucasian race, who called themselves God-fearing people, used the Bible to justify their bigotry and misdeeds. There was no compassion for blacks, only hatred and disgust. They spewed venomous and derogatory words, every chance they could, and took great pleasure in doing so. Apparently, they had no recollection of anything written in the Proverbs such as:

"The thoughts of the wicked are an
abomination to the Lord: but the words of
the pure are pleasant words."
(Proverbs 15:26 NIV).

They took scripture entirely out of context in proclaiming; they were God's chosen people as if they were the only ones.

While some may have allowed slaves the right to worship God, they refused to allow them to learn how to read out of fear that truth would be discovered. Fast-forward to modern times, and nothing has changed much. Gone are the days of slavery, Jim Crow laws, and segregation (supposedly), but there remains no compassion. There is still firm evidence of intolerance and contempt toward the black community or anyone who is nonwhite.

In my first book entitled *Will Somebody Please Listen,* I also touched base on the issues of racial divide in this country and how it is not a one-sided problem. I believe we all play a role in the matters that keep us from coming together in a united way. But in the year 2020, a lot has happened to change my viewpoint drastically.

Oh, I still believe we all play a part in the things which cause us to be divided; however, in that first book, I mentioned the fact there are many decent and good-hearted Caucasian people among us. By way of illustration, I gave a couple of examples I had with some white friends and their families while growing up in the small hick town of Maysville, Kentucky. Not long after that book release, I experienced a grave disappointment at the hands of the very people I honestly thought were legitimate. I grew up thinking they were some of the good guys and gals within the Caucasian race, but instead, I discovered some of them, too, had hidden feelings about the black community that amounted to disdain.

Today, I am uncertain. I don't know what to think, nor do I know who I can trust. I just know, for reasons that goes far beyond my ability to comprehend, my people and I are despised simply because we are different, and that is disturbing. Even more troubling is how well some can disguise their true feelings under the pretense of religion, but as I think back to my earlier point, a person's actual nature will surface sooner or later.

I hear the expressions of love by those I call into question now. Nevertheless, I do not see the authenticity of it. How can you love me, yet you do not see me (or my people) as your equal? How do you love me but fail to stand beside me or stand up against those who mistreat me or deny me certain rights and privileges because I am different from you?

Perhaps one of the most significant arguments in pointing out their hypocrisy is the position many of them take on pro-life. It is common among the Caucasian race (specifically white evangelicals) to express their displeasure with abortion; that is the ultimate no-no in their eyes. What I find to be ridiculous about being a strong advocate for pro-life is how they don't apply the same viewpoint toward all life. Pro-life, in its simplest definition, means a person is for life–period. So, if that is the case, then where are the voices of these so-called pro-life advocates when black men and women are senselessly and brutally killed? I presented this question to a person I have considered a lifelong friend who is white–and I could tell by his response that he didn't quite know what to think. I do not hold it against him, but I would be a liar if I said it doesn't bother me at all.

Imagine what impact they could have or what difference they could make if they would stand as firm against the killing of blacks (fully developed human beings, by the way) as they do for the killing of babies that haven't fully developed. Consider this: according to Wikipedia, in 2017, white evangelicals made up 17% of the American population, which was approximately 325,000,000 people. If you do the math, that means America had approximately 55,250,000 white evangelicals associated with the Christian religion's teachings. Now to give this thing some context, in 2016, a reported 80% of white evangelical voters came out to support the 45th President of the United States (by now, everyone knows who I am talking about, and I'll leave it at that). Let's assume America's population and the number of white evangelical voters in 2016 were very similar to 2017. If we tally up 80% of 55,250,000, that gives us 44,200,000 who supported the President, a number that has not decreased much in 2020, if at all.

So, what is the big deal? It is a huge deal because the 45th President despises movements like "Black Lives

Matter." He refuses to denounce white supremacists, and he continually stokes racial tension. Yet just over 44 million people who claim to be followers of Christ never challenge him on these matters. Without beating a dead horse into the ground, somewhere in that number are people who invited me to their church, listened to me preach, called me brother, and declared they love me (not just me but also my fellow African American brothers and sisters). All the while, they stand in strong support of a bigot and keep overwhelmingly silent on matters involving black lives.

I have heard several Caucasian colleagues try to dress down racism in America right now by stating the media is blowing things out of proportion. They want us to believe we have gotten beyond racism. Things are so much different and better in the relationship between our communities – which poses a huge problem because it is an insult to the black population's intelligence (or most anyway).

The media is not influencing our viewpoint! We possess the ability to clearly see for ourselves that things have not drastically changed. How dare they make such a claim when, thanks to modern technology, we see images of a white police officer, in Minneapolis Minnesota, kneeling on the neck of an African American man who is pleading with him to stop because he cannot breathe. Despite the victim's plea, the police officer maintained his position for eight full minutes until he took the man's life. There was absolutely no mercy, no compassion, nor any concern by the officer.

Media had nothing to do with what our eyes beheld in Atlanta, Georgia, as a white police officer shot and killed a black man who was in no way posing a threat to authorities. When the young man saw the officers were trying to apprehend him, he acted foolishly and attempted to run for it. But since when does running from the police require the use of lethal force? Media never shaped our thoughts over an incident that occurred in Brunswick, Georgia, when again, thanks to technology, the world witnessed the shooting of an unarmed black man while he was out for a jog. Two white men (one a former police officer) felt they had a right to make a citizen's arrest because they suspected the young man of breaking into homes in the community and robbing them.

I would be remiss if I failed to acknowledge the senseless killing of a young black lady in Kentucky by white police officers in the city of Louisville. She and her boyfriend were startled by officers breaking into their home in the middle of the night without announcing themselves, and the young man, attempting to protect his home, shot at the officers. As the police fired back, the young lady was struck and killed. Let me also not fail to mention the despicable shooting of an unarmed black man in Kenosha, Wisconsin, when police officers shot not once but seven times in the back of a man who, again, was walking away from them.

These are but a few of what were many incidents in 2020 that escalated the racial tension in this country; incidents in which full justice has yet to be served or denied altogether (as in the Kentucky shooting). And some of my Caucasian brothers in the ministry have the nerve to say they don't believe America has a racial problem or that media is blowing things out of proportion. Come on, man! They want us to feel everything is alright when it comes to racism, and the fact is – it's just not true!

What is even more insulting is many of the officials involved in such cases (i.e., state attorney generals, prosecuting attorneys, judges, police officers, etc.) are themselves members of a church. They are in the number of over 44 million white evangelicals, but very few seem to exhibit a character of righteousness; neither do they seem to have a conscience. Interesting is what the Bible says of such people and how they should conduct themselves:

> *"Consider carefully what you do, because you are not judging for man but for the Lord, who is with you whenever you give a verdict. Now let the fear of the Lord be upon you. Judge carefully, for with the Lord our God there is no injustice or partiality or bribery."*
> *(II Chronicles 19:6-7 NIV).*

Those are the words of Jehoshaphat as he appointed

judges in the land of Jerusalem. In essence, he was imploring them to be fair and righteous as public officials assigned to decide cases in court or as people who uphold the law. For that is the will of God, which is to be observed by all His people. Like much of the Bible teaching, it fails to be put into practice by those who claim to have such high regard for morals and Christian values.

Remember when I stated earlier how I find it unfortunate some do not know the significance of love? Well, here is what I mean by that. In I Peter 4:8, the apostle says,

"Above all, love each other deeply,
because love covers over a multitude of
sins." (NIV).

First, let me say that passage is not to be looked upon as permission to sin. But because we are sinful people, meaning, once again, we will have some character defects-then if we love right, it will cover over our flaws. Think of it like this; we are not going to have pure thoughts all the time, we are not going to make every right decision, we are not going to be able to prevent from having a slip of the tongue, we are not going to avoid hurting some people and so forth. However, if we understand the significance of love, in that it must be the paramount quality which is to shine in the life of every believer because it is the core of the nature of God Himself; and if we display such love toward one another, then it will make up for our shortcomings. So, when a church and its members fail to exhibit God's core nature, which is love that includes mercy, justice, compassion, righteousness, forgiveness, etc., that is the real hypocrisy.

In the above cases, no official immediately claimed they made a mistake or attempted to apologize to the victims' families. Instead, many of them played the role of victim. And yet again, I must emphasize, these are the type of people who love to boast of their religious affiliation. Why blame anyone for wanting no part in the church when hypocritical people of this magnitude are members?

A Misplaced Priority

I suppose once you begin reading this chapter, it will appear to be an extension of my case against hypocritical behavior. Perhaps in some regard, it is, but I entitled it *"A Misplaced Priority"* because ultimately, I believe this is the catalyst behind the hypocrisy of the previous chapter. Jesus says something recorded in Matthew and Luke, which sets the stage for this argument:

> *"For where your treasure is, there your*
> *heart will be also."*
> *(Matthew 6:21; Luke 12:34 NIV).*

A person's heart is the place in which the thing they value most is stored. According to Jesus' teaching, whatever a man or woman treasures most upon this earth, their heart will follow. If we take this concept a step further, it can also be said that where the heart is, there lie the person's priorities. And judging by what we see amongst several church members today – their heart is with the world, which is to say their priorities are worldly centered or worldly connected.

Given John's teaching, that is a conflict of interest for those who consider themselves to be children of God, as he writes:

> *"Do not love the world or anything in the*
> *world. If anyone loves the world, the love*
> *of the Father is not in him. For*
> *everything in the world – the cravings of*
> *sinful man, the lust of his eyes and the*
> *boasting of what he has and does – comes*
> *not from the Father but from the world."*

> *(I John 2:15-16 NIV).*

Please understand, what John is saying has nothing to do with being unable to appreciate the beauty, splendor, and resources of the earth and heavens. On the contrary, he is implying we must not become so attached to this life on earth that we have no desire or passion for a life with God. Because if we have no zeal for a life with God, then neither will we have any zeal in striving to live by His standards. This world is a system of man-made governments and societies, with some good and some not so good. Thus, John's words challenge us to understand we are not to love the world to the point we are more attached to the systems of man's organizations than we are to God and heaven.

Finally, the world is also full of evil, prideful, and rebellious people. So, once more, with John's teaching in mind, we must not love to remain in the company of such or desire to be associated with them in any capacity. As a genuine follower of Christ, there should be a yearning to come out from among people of this caliber.

Nonetheless, there lies another colossal dilemma. It seems as if many, who profess to know scripture, have not given much consideration to John's teaching. There are far too many who love more about the world than they do of God or heaven. It is truly becoming a problem of grand proportions, as it prevents church members from standing out as righteous people. I frequently find myself telling the congregation(s) in which I am blessed to lead – that there must be something different about us whenever we claim allegiance to Christ and his church. We must live by a different set of values, a different way of thinking, a different belief, and a different set of priorities. We should dare not be influenced by the world. Instead, it should be the other way around – we should influence the world! The power and impact we can have as God's people is enormous; if only we would focus on the things which are most important to our walk of life.

As I write, all eyes are on the state of Georgia and its upcoming senate run-off election on January 5, 2021. Two critical seats in the U.S. Senate are up for grabs, and much of America is on edge in anticipation of who shall win these seats. Both sides, Democrats and Republicans, desperately want their candidates to win for different reasons. Personally, I have never been one to get deep into politics. In fact, I cannot stand it because I hate the bickering and underhanded stuff that goes on in that arena.

There are some good and bad in the ideology of both major political parties. It is not what they believe or disbelieve that bothers me; it is the people's character.

I despise that this nation is called the United States of America when nothing is united. Politicians in America, specifically those of the Republican party, truly do not put the country first and try to work together for the greater good of our nation; instead, it is always about what is in the best interest of a select group of people, typically the wealthy. Of course, this is not to say the Democrats do not have their issues because they do, which is why I despise anything about politics because no politician can genuinely be trusted regardless of party affiliation. You may be thinking this is not an American problem; instead, this is happening worldwide. I have no doubt it is, but I'm not writing about what is going on in the world – my focus is right here on what is supposed to be the greatest nation on earth.

Once upon a time, at least as far as I can remember, church folk (pastors in particular) did their absolute best to refrain from engaging in political conversations or politics period. I guess it can be said in the technical sense it was just part of honoring the *separation of church and state* rule. Without going into a scholastic definition, the idea behind *separation of church and state* simply means there is no place for the combination of religion and the activities of our country's governance.

Despite what government and its officials try to portray when discussing how this country was built upon Christian principles or when speaking of their morals and values, the truth of the matter, it is just a façade. They want you to believe the two entities can co-exist, but in reality, they have no part with one another. Satan has a strong presence and an even stronger influence in the political arena; therefore, if one thinks they can push an agenda where Satan dwells while standing on moral values and biblical principles, they need to think again. I know what you're probably thinking about now. The nerve of this guy to say such a thing, and what is his basis for saying it?

Well, how about we start with the fact the political arena is full of deceitful, selfish, cut-throat people who *lie, cheat, steal,* and in some cases, *kill* to get what they want. That sounds like characteristics of Satan to me per my understanding of what the Bible teaches about him. And so, you tell me, does that seem like an environment that will welcome anyone who pushes for love, unity, honesty, equality, etc.? I don't think so! But in saying that, it does not mean I will not support an individual who chooses to step into such an arena with a strong desire to make a difference or to put forth a valiant effort to change the environment. Neither should anyone consider them-selves true believers and fail to support one of our own who takes on this task. We should always support any person who seeks to do the work of God, which is why I draw attention to the senate race.

One of the candidates representing the Democratic side is a respected black pastor who happens to be the under-shepherd of Dr. Martin Luther King's old stomp-ing ground, Ebenezer Baptist. I don't know the brother personally, but I know of him, and this was long before he catapulted onto the political scene. I know enough to say with confidence that he shares the dreams and vision that Dr. King once had; he is a man, who is in many ways, carrying on the legacy of MLK. That means he is an advocate of civil rights; he has compassion for the poor and middle-class people, and he sides with justice for all.

His campaign is currently running on the idea that he will fight to gain healthcare for every American. He will push for police reform in lieu of the recent string of incidents suggesting that police brutality is way out of control. He wants minimum wages to increase as well as college students to be able to have affordable education. He is a person who believes in the constitution, but just not in the way some uphold it. Based on his credentials, his passion, his goals, and most of all, his spirit, you cannot help but love the man and what he is trying to do. That is if you are genuinely a believer of God's righteous principles!

Again, not everyone in the political arena is a genuine believer, which is no big deal. The big deal is those who say they are and seem to have a special interest in what's going on in that arena. Why is that a big deal, you ask? Because sadly, their interest very seldom appears to be motivated by biblical teaching, or their interest never seems to be in a person like the candidate mentioned above.

I find it absurd that as a fellow Christian or fellow believer, you would not be anything but proud and supportive of one of your own having the courage to stand in Satan's den bringing the fight to him on his turf. If you are a person who claims to walk with integrity and to maintain Christian values and principles – why is it that you would not dare come out in strong support of someone who holds to those same values and principles? In this case, it should not matter what the individual's party affiliation is or what color their skin is; what should matter is they are standing on the side of righteousness. So, why would you not be elated about that?

Don't worry; I'll answer that for you! In a nutshell, it is because your priorities are misplaced. You talk godly principles, but you do not value them; instead, you value political principles. Why? Because somewhere deep in the language of the constitution lies your protection or something that supports your livelihood. In all likelihood, your interest is not in the greater good for all people, but what's right for you, the individual, or your family. You do not want to see this country succeed, for you're only interested in your success, well-being, benefits, etc.

For instance: why is there a huge resistance to having healthcare for every person in this nation? Why, as a child of God, would you not want that? In 2010, while in college, I wrote a paper on what is really behind healthcare opposition. Media reports claimed the number one concern was cost; how would it get paid for, or who would cover the expense? In all fairness, that was a legitimate concern, but I genuinely believe there were several underlying apprehensions – one of which was greed.

When I wrote that paper, the Affordable Care Act (a.k.a. Obamacare) was not yet in existence, but the players on Capitol Hill were in a tizzy trying to ensure it would never see the light of day; that such a thing would never be signed into law. And I could never understand the reason behind their strong opposition! It just did not make sense when, according to world rankings, the United States was listed in the top five of the wealthiest nations. Of course, at the same time, the U.S. was also ranked nineteenth on a list of countries that had the best healthcare. But that only moved me to be more inquisitive about the matter. How could there be such a vast discrepancy; how could we be one of the wealthiest, most powerful nations in the world yet could not afford to make healthcare available to all our citizens? I concluded this: It was the greed (still is) of insurance companies and the politicians who protect them and the greed of you who protect the politicians that protect the insurance companies.

Why perpetrate by flaunting the idea of wanting righteousness to prevail, but at the end of the day, there is not a righteous bone in your body? How can it be if you are not willing to be in support of a person who pursues righteousness and who wants to hold people accountable that should be? Does not the Bible tell us:

"Look not every man on his own things,
but every man also on the things of others.
Let this mind be in you, which was also in
Christ Jesus…?" (Philippians 2:4-5 KJV).

Of course it does, so then, why do you continue to look out only for yourself – oh ye who claim to have moral standards? It is said of some scholars that the world is too needful and too desperate for any believer to be focused upon himself. Every believer is needed to reach the lost and lonely, the shut-ins and helpless, the hungry and cold, the sinful and doomed of his community, city, and country. Every believer does not need to be thinking about his own things but on the things of others.

Speaking of doomed, right now, we are dealing with a global pandemic called coronavirus or Covid-19. It was recently reported that here in the United States, we have suffered the loss of more people from this virus than all the deaths during WWII. The number of people who are getting sick and dying from this dreaded disease increases by the day. Many healthcare officials say it is getting out of control, and the one thing that could help control it is a simple wearing of a mask. But people are refusing to comply. Why? Because politicians-the very same ones who are quick to tell you about their Christian values-have politicized the idea of mask-wearing. Many are on record as being vehemently opposed to shutting down establishments for economic purposes (which I understand to a degree). Still, they refuse to mandate that all people wear masks until a vaccine is made available to thwart this pandemic. Where is the concern or compassion for our fellow man? Why is the priority of our leaders (including many pastors) centered on keeping the economy open instead of keeping the people safe?

This brings to mind something my professor used to say while taking New Testament classes: "People don't care about how much you know until they know about how much you care." Gone are the days in which you can pretty much talk your way through anything. We are now living in a time where actions do speak more than words. You can stand up and talk about your values, principles, beliefs and make all the promises you want, but unless you show it, only a fool will believe what it is you are trying to sell. There are just way too many supposed Christian folk and politicians claiming to have Christian values. Evidence strongly shows that your only value (or priority) is in the world, which ultimately means it is in your desires. And you who dare to be this way are smearing the church's image.

Church Is Not an
Organization

I believe one of the biggest misconceptions about the church is how it should operate. Many are functioning as though they are an organization, but the church is no such thing. It is an organism foremost–as it is the spiritual body of Christ. The church is one unit with many parts that must depend upon one another if the unit is to operate efficiently and effectively. And even as the local church reflects the universal church (supposedly), the same concept must apply for the reflection to be accurate. Just as all parts of our physical bodies depend on each other, so does the spiritual body of Christ rely on all its members to work in unison.

Imagine how chaotic it would be if our hands, feet, mouth, ears, eyes, and nose each failed to work together. Just think of the degree of difficulty it would cause us as individuals if our eyes saw food that looked delicious and our nose, in cooperation, was drawn to the pleasant aroma, creating a desire to eat the wonderful looking meal, but our mouth refused to oblige. Sounds a bit crazy, I know! Yet, those would be the issues we would likely face if our body parts did not work with one another.

Thankfully, we do not have to be concerned with anything of the sort because Paul reminds us,

"... God has arranged the parts in the body, every one of them, just as He wanted them to be." (I Corinthians 12:18 NIV).

The result: no body part can say to the other, "I don't need you!" For, the way in which all parts of the body were arranged was so they could all function in unison. Say what you want about God, but there is one thing I guarantee no person can say about Him in a negative sense, and that is–He does not create confusion. Order and unity are synonymous with God's name! Within an organization, on the other hand, that is not always the case.

From 1997 to 2009, while living at home in Maysville, Kentucky, I worked for a prominent Japanese industry that specialized in the production of automotive parts. Initially, the company started out making *car audio* parts, but a few years later, it expanded and began producing *car engine* parts. In fact, the expansion made it necessary to construct a separate building, although it was literally next door. Consequently, two entities existed on the same property, under the same company name, but were not co-dependent.

To go a step further, this Japanese company has several other plants established throughout the world. Each facility operates under one primary name; however, they are an entity all on their own and are not dependent upon another. Naturally, there are some things they try to have in common, such as the type of benefits they offer to their employees. Nevertheless, the success of these facilities is not contingent upon the success of the other. There is no serious concern the organization will close its

85

doors if one department fails. Neither is the organization's overall efficiency and effectiveness dependent upon each department's cohesion: only their contribution is what matters.

This is not how the church can operate and expect to be relevant. I will agree there are moments in which it must conduct some business comparable to an organization. However, the harmony in which its members operate determines the church's success or failures. Unity is everything in the eyes of God, and so should it be with those of us who call ourselves children of God. One of my favorite scripture texts is Psalm 133, as the writer declares:

> *"Behold, how good and how pleasant it is*
> *for brethren to dwell together in unity! It is*
> *like the precious ointment upon the head,*
> *that ran down upon the beard, even*
> *Aarons beard: that went down to the skirts*
> *of his garments; as the dew of Hermon,*
> *and as the dew that descended upon the*
> *mountains of Zion: for there the Lord*

commanded the blessing, even life

evermore." (KJV).

While there are only three verses in that psalm, there is a wealth of teaching. But so I can stay on point with this message, I will just sum up what the psalmist suggests as it applies to a gathering of God's people.

The effectiveness of a church hinges on having strong pastoral leadership and cooperative membership. In a sense, these are two different entities within the church body. Still, if they do not exist and work together simultaneously, the church will not successfully draw others to Christ and bring them into the sweet communion of discipleship – which is its mandate.

The same can be said of every facet of the church. Every member must get along and work together, and every preacher must find a way to co-exist. All leadership needs to be on one accord. There must be harmony or cohesion between all parts of the body, from the most important down to the least important. That is not to say everyone should think, feel, and act the same way. It just implies we must do our absolute best to ensure we are functioning as one unit.

As a pastor, I have experienced plenty of upsetting moments in watching various members of my leadership team go at each other's throats over nonsense. Instead of seeing how important it is to function as a unit that there may have to be some sacrifices for such to happen; some are only concerned about their ideas, suggestions, and feelings. The really disturbing thing is to see disagreements and disputes occur in front of people they're supposed to be leading or in front of a guest. If you are looking for a quick way to destroy the church's image, look no further than the unruly actions of members who cannot co-exist.

My pastor used to say unto me: "We are not called to be successful; we are called to be faithful – but it's in our faithfulness that we become successful." For a long time, I never quite knew what he meant, and then one day, it hit me. God has no concern with whether we be individually successful (or not) in terms of financial gain, achievements, accolades, etc. His main concern is that we are faithful to His cause, which, somewhere at the top of the list, involves us living in harmony and love. Scripture urges us to,

"Do everything without complaining or
arguing, so that you may become
blameless and pure children of God
without fault in a crooked and depraved
generation, in which you shine like stars in
the universe as you hold out the word of
life..." (Philippians 2:14-16 NIV).

Murmuring and disputes only lead to turmoil and divisiveness, which stands in total contrast to why we are to gather as believers. It is imperative we understand, since we cannot see God, our commitment to Him is shown through the relationship we have with one another. When we are faithful in following His commands, statutes, principles, and so forth, that is what garners ultimate success. And of course, the opposite is true when we do not!

Members disputing amongst themselves are examples of what may go on inside individual churches, but

let's consider what goes on between various congregations. Another disturbing thing I find is how so many
local churches isolate themselves from the rest of the
body. After 24 years of being in ministry, I still cannot
wrap my mind around this! You may be a member of a
Baptist denomination, but you need your brother and sisters of the Methodist, Presbyterian, Lutheran, Pentecostal
faiths as well. You may be a member of a mega-church,
but it does not mean you are to have no affiliation with
rural country churches. You may attend a church where
the congregation is all-white, but it does not qualify you
to withdraw from fellowshipping with a church with an
all-black congregation (or whatever the church's ethnic-
ity may be). You may be part of a church full of highly
educated and well-to-do people, but does that mean you
should not connect with a church whose members are
less educated or less prosperous?

If the spiritual body of Christ is one, such must be
reflected in the actions of its members. How can we serve
the same God, read the same Bible, claim to have the
same beliefs, and yet have dissension amongst ourselves?

How can we have different viewpoints about how the church should function along with our responsibility as members if we share the same spirit? Am I missing something when I read the words of Paul in Ephesians as he declares:

"There is one body, and one Spirit, even
as ye are called in one hope of your
calling; One Lord, one faith, one baptism,
One God and Father of all, who is above
all, and through all, and in you all?"
(Ephesians 4:4-6 KJV).

Is Paul suggesting in some underlying fashion that what he states in Ephesians is only applicable to a select group of people? Of course not, for then he would be hypocritical in his teaching! After all, Paul stated elsewhere in scripture that God shows no favoritism with people *(Romans 2:11)*. So, the only conclusion which makes logical sense is when a church is operating like an organization instead of an organism, it cannot live up to its expectations.

What has always been troubling for me when it

comes to organizations is how their priority (or purpose) is to look out for themselves with the heads of the company benefiting before anyone else. An organization most usually lacks compassion or feelings; it is only concerned with results. If you are a member of any association, be it sports, entertainment, business, etc., and are not producing on a level expected of you. In that case, chances are you won't be around much longer as you serve no purpose to the group. They do not care about whatever problems may exist, which could prevent your productivity; they are not concerned that you have a family who is a priority in your eyes. Bottom line: when you don't produce, you will get reduced – plain and simple. If this mindset is permitted to enter the church (and it is), it becomes quite damaging to the work we have been called to do as believers.

You're now thinking, come on, preacher. Isn't all this a bit extreme? I do not think so! Oh, I'm not suggesting the church is as blatant with their heartless actions; no doubt, they are a little more subtle. But being subtle does not make it any less hurtful. I have heard strong reports (from reliable sources) about questionable methods practiced in mega-churches pertaining to offering and tithes. However, before I say anything further, let me reiterate that what I am about to convey is only speculation and nothing I can confirm. While I have confidence in the sources I received, I have not witnessed their claims firsthand. Let me also reiterate, I have established at the very beginning of this book that the basis for my arguments stems from personal experience, conversations with fellow ministry leaders, and observing people's behavior in the religious arena. I am providing in support of my arguments a simple viewpoint and opinion to which, I believe, counts for something – considering the length of time I have been in ministry.

Having gotten that out of the way, now let me say: it was told to me from a pastor friend who visited a prominent megachurch in Atlanta that the congregation was seated in accordance with their financial contribution (I emphasize was because this practice may be done away with now). Those who contributed more were privileged to sit in the front of the arena, while those who sit in the upper arena (or balcony) contributed less.

When I first heard this, I was in shock! I questioned the brother several times about this matter because I genuinely thought he was kidding. But he assured me it was no joke. Apparently, this applied to members only. If you were a guest, you could sit with whatever guest invited you. However, if you were not invited, the balcony was your likely destination.

If what he told me was true, and I have no reason to believe it wasn't, imagine this process. Imagine you have been a member of this church for several years and have been blessed to be a top-tier contributor. Therefore, the only seat you have known has been in front of the arena (only feet away from the pulpit). Yet suddenly, through circumstances beyond your control, your income has drastically changed, and you are no longer able to contribute like before. I want you to think of the embarrassment it would likely create.

Here you are, in what is supposed to be God's house to hear a word from the Lord, and more than likely, the message which is going to resonate for some, is the whispers involving your financial situation that was generated by where you are now sitting. I don't know about you, but I would feel insulted and hurt by the unnecessary attention. We do not go to church to have attention drawn to us; instead, the attention is supposed to be on the preacher's message. Indeed, this sounds like a ridiculous scenario, but I have accepted that these are the types of things that can happen when church is run like an organization rather than an organism.

Consider this, is it any wonder how even within some establishments lies isolation of its members? I mean, after all, if they are not willing to follow the plan of God for the whole body, how can they expect that things will be okay with them individually? I believe strongly that who and what we are will be seen in all aspects of our living. If we are harmonious people, it will show through actions of love, compassion, and mercy for one another; on the flip side, if we are divisive people, we will indeed lack such actions.

A Failure to Apply

Now, I want to talk about something that hits home with all of us connected to the church in some capacity. Without question, the leading cause behind the damaging image of the universal church is what goes on with the membership of our local congregations (whether it be clergy, members, etc.). But it would be so unfair of me to leave the door open, suggesting that only a few are responsible, or some within local congregations are perhaps a little better than others because that is not true. Two things put such an idea to rest quickly, and both are found in scripture. In the "B" part of Romans 3:12, Paul declares:

>*"...there is no one who does good, not*
>*even one." (NIV).*

A few verses later, Paul says,

>*"For all have sinned, and come short of*
>*the glory of God..." (Romans 3:23 KJV).*

If you understand what Paul is doing at this juncture of his letter to the Romans; you know he is merely closing the door on anyone's belief that they can look at another person's flaws, as though they have none and perhaps feel as if they are superior (or better).

In the first chapter of Romans, he lays out a case against the Gentiles, claiming they are guilty in every conceivable way you can imagine, as they have: rejected God, are filled with darkness in their hearts, have become fools, follow the desires of their own heart over what God desires for them and much more. Basically, they relish in sin, which causes them to do unnatural things. When you get to the second chapter, Paul shifts attention to the moralist (people who judge others because of a failure to live by their standard or expectation). He clarifies that when a person judges another, they condemn themselves since they do the same things for which they judge others.

One of the big talking points in church circles to-day centers around a controversial subject matter known as homosexuality. It is a topic that has always drawn the ire of religionist everywhere. Now, in light of a 2015 ruling which enabled same-sex marriage to be legally recognized in all fifty states in the U.S., it is causing an uproar. In watching the response of many of my colleagues and various other clergy and members within the religious arena, I must say I am a bit surprised by what appears to be an overreaction. You would think by such a ruling, the world has already come to an end, or better yet, you would think it was the worst decision ever made by our lawmakers. I don't think there is any question, it was a horrible decision, but the world is not coming to an end – yet!

Now, please do not misconstrue what I am saying. I will be the first to declare that I do not condone homosexuality, and I stand with my fellow brothers and sisters who are disappointed that such a ruling could come to fruition. My surprise at the overreaction stems from the idea that many seem to have lost sight of what homosexuality is. It is a sin that happens to be no greater or no lesser than any other act of sin! If I have read my Bible correctly and my understanding is accurate, God does not differentiate sin. So, why do we? If God despises all sin equally, then why don't we do the same? Are we to believe it is okay to hate the homosexual as many seem to be guilty of doing and elevate ourselves above them because we are heterosexual? If that is our stance, it is one of absurdity!

I despise the act of homosexuality, but I cannot despise the individual because if so, I have no choice but to despise myself since I am no better off. Allow me now to pick back up on a discussion I started in chapter one. I have done many terrible things in my lifetime – none of which are anything to be proud of. I have *lied*, *cheated*, *fornicated*, *stolen*, and even been involved in *adultery*. You cannot begin to know the embarrassment and shame I feel at this moment admitting such, but it is necessary to prevent coming across as a person holier-than-thou. Thus far, I have exposed a lot of wrongdoing by church folk, and I have to man-up by confessing I have played a role in this as well; I am no less flawed than all the people I have drawn attention to!

Thankfully, the things I have alluded to are no longer a part of my life today. Nonetheless, I still sin because sin is a matter of the heart and mind and not just a person's actions. So, what I am telling you is while I no longer act out, sometimes I think about sinful things I ought not to be thinking about.

Show me someone who never has a negative thought or never takes a second look at a person of the opposite sex a bit too long, and I will show you someone who is in denial of sin. And if they are in denial, then obviously, there is no truth in them. John said, *"If we say that we have no sin, we deceive ourselves…"* He goes on to say,

> *"If we say that we have not sinned, we*
> *make Him (God) a liar, and His word is*
> *not in us." (I John 1:8,10 KJV).*

There is not a person among us who can help what pops up in their mind. We indeed have influence over what we allow to stay in our minds, but what enters is beyond our control, and whether we admit it or not, those thoughts contribute to our sinful nature. Therefore, as we swing back around to Paul's point: If you are going to judge a person to the point of condemning them for their sinful actions, then you must be aware you are condemning yourself also – because there is none good!

Many of us like to hide under the umbrella of religious teaching, specifically those of us that practice the Christian faith. We are quick to fall back on the promises of God and what scripture confirms about our position with Him as children of faith. We are quick to convey who we are and what we believe. Oh, and one of our favorites is proclaiming the blood of Christ and how we are covered by such as though that makes us invincible. But in the latter half of Romans chapter 2, Paul has a word for the religionist. There, he talks to the Jews; however, the principle applies to all who call themselves Christian.

Paul points out that being a Jew (or Christian) is not a matter of race, culture, or any proclamation; it is a matter of conduct. What significance is there to claim all that we do and embrace the law or standards of God but refuse to live by them? What benefit is there in reading and studying the scripture but never conforming to what is taught? Even James teaches:

"Do not merely listen to the word, and so deceive yourselves. Do what it says..."
(James 1:22 NIV).

The Apostle Paul leaves no stone unturned in laying out his argument that not a soul on earth has anything to be confident of when it comes to the matter of righteousness. We all fall short of God's glory, and there is one issue we all have in common which causes such. Simply put, we fail to conform by failing to comply. In layman's terms, we do not act according to what the Bible teaches because we do not yield to its teaching or do not apply its teaching (at least not consistently).

When I was attending Carver Bible College, I took a course entitled *Bible Study Methods*. The objective was to provide students with the art and science to study the Bible properly; basically, it was an introductory class to hermeneutics. During that class, the emphasis was placed

on three main phases of Bible study: *Observation, Interpretation,* and *Application.* Our instructor used the
following analogy in the observation phase: whenever
we read the Bible, we should approach it like a detective
observing a crime scene. In other words, look for nothing
but clues.

For example: whenever you see the word "therefore," always ask yourself what is it there for because it
indicates a continuing thought. The question is, what
thought? Look for repetitive words, capitalized words,
italicized words, so on and so forth. Once you feel that
you have gathered up enough evidence, then move to the
next phase of interpretation. That is basically when you
start putting all the pieces of the puzzle together but never
attempt to put the puzzle together without first having the
pieces. Some like to bypass the observation phase and go
straight to interpretation, which typically lends to why
scripture gets taken out of context. After we are careful
to follow phases 1 and 2, then comes the all-important
phase 3. However, I don't think I have to tell you; this
phase becomes our neutralizer, or perhaps I should say,

this is where our ineffectiveness shows up the most.

It is often said the Bible is a living word, and it has the power to transform lives. Well, for that to happen, the instructions it conveys must be applied to our lives, not just some of it and not only sometimes. If we are unwilling to yield to all of God's word, allowing it to be our guide, and if we pick-n-choose which times we feel like being Christ-like, we cannot expect change. Consider this illustration: We cannot adhere to the teachings of Psalm 107:1 and ignore the teachings of I Thessalonians 5:18. Both texts instruct us to give thanks to God, but in the I Thessalonians passage, emphasis must be placed on the first three words,

*"**In everything give** thanks: for this is the will of God in Christ Jesus concerning you" (KJV).*

You see, some are quick to thank God when things are going well and hesitant to do so when things are not so well. But Paul reminds the believer that no matter the circumstances in our life – we are always to give thanks. Likewise, we cannot just thank Him on Sunday (during worship service); instead, our expression of gratitude must be continual. For even though our circumstances may change, God does not change; He is always good to us and worthy of our constant praise!

Failure to consistently apply all of God's word to our lives is an indictment of every person regardless of who you are or your church affiliation. We want to be righteous people when it is convenient for us or when it looks good. But come judgment day, we will be in for a rude awakening if we do not correct that error now. If we are going to address the wrongdoings of homosexuality, we also had better address:

➢ The issue of people shacking up
➢ Lying to save face
➢ Deceiving people for personal gain
➢ The issue of divorce because of irreconcilable differences
➢ Adulterous relationships
➢ Unethical behavior
➢ And much, much more!

Some of us need to be careful about having these

self-righteous attitudes that are on display. I will ask again; however, please do not misconstrue what I am saying. I am not implying we should turn our back on any type of sin. We must address it; we are obligated to do so. I am only trying to suggest we do not focus on one sin as being more egregious than another, and neither should we condemn anyone for their sinful behavior if we do not wish to be condemned. In the words of a popular song we used to sing on Sunday mornings: "It's not my brother, nor my sister, but it's me O Lord, standing in the need of prayer." Time is being spent looking at the speck of dust in others' eyes while failing to see the plank in our own eyes. When we fail to apply all of God's word to our lives, we are equally detrimental to the church's image, as are the atheist preacher, wishy-washy church member, the hypocrites, and all others.

Taking Scripture Out of Context

The last damaging thing to the church's image I wish to address is the confusion created behind scripture being taken out of context. I could have included this topic in chapter one, but I feel the need to spotlight it separately because I do not see it as a problem with false preachers only. As mentioned during the introduction, no one has cornered the market on God's word, which means no person has a fully developed understanding of everything written in the Holy Scripture. Therefore, all who teach the Bible are bound to take passages out of context occasionally.

The level of one's understanding will likely determine the frequency in which this happens, but I don't believe any man or woman has avoided ever taking a text out of context in some measure. I am sure I have done so and probably will continue–but never intentionally. If I am aware I have done such or if it is brought to my attention, I have absolutely no qualms about apologizing and declaring I made a mistake or perhaps misread the text. For nothing concerns me more, as a preacher, than being guilty of mishandling the word of God and thus misleading His people.

With that being said, I do take issue with the brother or sister who does not share the same concern. Some preachers or teachers of the Bible are either too comfortable with themselves and what they teach or too stubborn to accept they could be wrong about what they are teaching. From what I have seen, it appears to be a little of both. Also, pride seems to play a role for some. Some cannot stand the thought of their congregations becoming aware they do not know everything there is to know about scripture. And that thought process creates pride and prevents them from having any concern of misleading their congregations. They would rather chance deceiving a congregation than chancing the assembly finding out about their lack of understanding.

Not only that, but it also inhibits the ability for them to sit in the company of other ministers to reason together. I love sitting around other clergy members and listening to their perspectives on various texts in the scripture because I accept that I do not know it all, and I could learn something that will help my congregation. At the same time, I hope the company in which I sit feels the same way and don't have the mindset that they can never be taught something from the likes of me – perhaps because I am not on their level scholastically or because they are senior to me, in terms of experience in preaching.

It is amazing how some preachers love to quote Proverbs 27:17, which says,

"As iron sharpens iron, so one person
sharpens another." (NIV).

Yet, some of the very ones who quote this passage only prefer to do the sharpening and not be sharpened. I speak

111

from experience on this matter! Approximately three years ago (2017), I had a disagreement with a colleague from Kentucky who told me I was going straight to hell. This brother is someone I had great respect for because he was friends with my pastor and incredibly supportive of me after I had acknowledged my call into the ministry (not to mention he is several years older). He always offered encouragement and allowed me to preach at his church several times. From that, we began to bond, and once I became pastor, we became good friends. But after a while, I started noticing how he was from the old school of thought and unashamedly stuck in his ways.

He decided to condemn me to hell because he found out that since relocating to Georgia, where I now pastor in Jackson (Butts County) – I have an associate minister who happens to be female. This is taboo in the Baptist denomination, at least with many of the old guards. I was told by a mutual friend that he could not wait for my return to Kentucky because he had a few words for me (we hadn't spoken much after I relocated). As it turned out, he did indeed have some words for me! When I asked him on what grounds he was making this charge – he used I Corinthians 14:34 as his defense, which states:

"Let your women keep silence in the churches: for it is not permitted unto them to speak; but they are commanded to be under obedience, as also saith the law."
(KJV).

Here is the problem: when you lift that one verse out of its context, you take away the high esteem with which Christ and the New Testament hold women. First, the central focus of I Corinthians 14 is on the speaking of tongues. Paul mentions this matter because some women were abusing the gift of tongues and the predictive element of prophecy. Paul's charge is for the women to calm down and keep quiet, to bring things into order. The passage is directed to the local problem of the Corinthians and to any other church where not just women but any person is found abusing the gifts of tongues and the predictive element of prophecy.

This principle applies to every one of us today, but it just so happened the women of Paul's day (specifically those of Corinth) were the ones who needed to be addressed when Paul pens this letter. That verse did not indicate that women are forbidden to participate and share their gifts in the church (including the gift of preaching). However, for the sake of argument, let's say it was. If so, what is the big deal? Is this a salvation issue? Are women going to hell for doing so? Will members of the church go to hell for listening to them? Does it warrant condemning any male pastor for having a female associate? The answer is a resounding *"no"* to all the above! If anything, it is a matter of being out of order, but that is no more out of order than letting a known homosexual be the choir leader, of which he was guilty.

Before you take offense to what I just said, please be sure you first understand the point I am trying to make. I am not speaking ill-will of his (now former) choir member; I am merely pointing out something I mentioned in the previous chapter regarding double standards. We cannot pick-n-choose what battles we want to fight as soldiers in God's army, or we cannot spotlight some sins while turning our back on others. And we most definitely need to avoid taking scripture out of context to support our personal arguments or feelings. If I am out of order, and if someone can plainly show me how by way of sound teaching, I will not hesitate to ask for God's forgiveness and repent. But I suspect God has a problem with us for things much worse than a woman preaching His divine word, and I would say taking the text out of context is one such thing.

Listen! How about we start focusing on the big picture. Time is of the essence and too precious to be wasted on meaningless debates and disagreements. Every moment we spend trying to prove our knowledge of scripture, and every moment we spend squabbling over who's wrong or right, it is a moment we miss out on promoting the image of the church. How so, because we are providing a picture of discord, which is causing some to look upon the people of God with contempt. When we spend time trying to teach people something about the Bible that we are not sure of, we lose credibility and respect. And the more these things occur, the more likely people will be reluctant to ever have anything to do with the church.

All Is Not Hopeless

How many of you are thinking *WOW* at this point? Given what has been said from chapters 1-7, is there any reason to have hope for the church? I mean, how is it to thrive with all these issues? If no person is good and the real church is not a building but a collective group of messed up people, doesn't this cause concern that the church's existence may be in jeopardy? The answer is no! Remember that what Jesus declares in Matthew 16:18 suggests the church will not be overcome, not that it will not be attacked or face grave challenges. Nonetheless, I can see how such a concern might evolve along with others; but before you give them any credence, allow me to help you dispel the idea because those who are pure at heart have every reason to cling to hope!

Here now is where I John 1:9 becomes invaluable. The text says,

> *"If we confess our sins, he is faithful and just to forgive us our sins, and to cleanse us from all unrighteousness." (KJV).*

First, let us consider the word confess. By acknowledging our sin, we simply demonstrate that we agree with God about our life's condition; we are not living in denial. Secondly, the word sin is indicative of missing the mark. John declares that we must show ourselves to be in agreement with God that we miss the mark on everything involving acts of righteousness. Every day we must make this acknowledgment while asking God to forgive us for all we say, do, and think that is contrary to His divine will and way.

The all-important next step is to put forth a concerted effort to do better and turn away from those things that cause us to miss the mark of righteousness (i.e., lying, negative thinking, selfishness, greed, narcissism, etc.). When we fail, as we shall, there must be remorse, and then, to use another axiom, we need to get back on the horse and attempt to ride it again. That means returning to or resume an activity you previously failed at, had difficulty with, or which has formerly caused you harm and try to overcome. The reason I say all is not lost for the pure at heart is because they are the ones who adhere to John's teaching, who genuinely want to do the right things, and are under conviction when they don't.

Shortly after I got saved, about two years later, I had a major setback! I gave in to a weakness which, afterward, had me feeling extreme guilt. It was causing severe mental stress because I was doing so well in my new walk, and then all-of-a-sudden, it felt like I had let God down, and there was no mercy left for me. I was ready to give up! Satan had me just where he wanted, and he almost succeeded in swaying me to turn completely away from making any attempt to have a relationship with the Lord ever again, not because I had no desire, but because I was starting to feel it couldn't be done. If it were not for a conversation between my stepmother and me, let's just say things would be a lot different for me today (and not good).

I won't go into details about how the conversation got started, but in sharing with her, what I had done, she could see a heavy conviction was upon me. She let me talk for as long as I needed to, and then she proceeded to ask a question that sort of bothered me as I did not think it was appropriate at the moment. The question was, "How do you know when you are saved?" With how I was feeling, that was the last thing I wanted to be talking about, but out of respect, I answered, "I don't know!" What she said next resonated in a way words cannot explain!

She said, "When you do wrongful things and are convicted, it is a great indicator your life has changed, and you have been saved. Otherwise, if you were still the same old unsaved person, you would have no problems with what you have done."

As I contemplated those words and began reflecting, it was amazing how right she was. The old me never gave a second thought about anything I did wrong. In my mind, I wasn't. It was just all about having fun.

When God begins to do a new thing in us, little do we realize how such involves punishment whenever we get out of step with His will for our lives. The Hebrew writer reminds us that God is treating us as His children whenever we find ourselves being disciplined. When there is no discipline, it is a sign of illegitimacy. My step-mother's words provided renewed hope as I began to recognize God was simply spanking me, as a father will do to a child he loves. Her words also made me realize this Christian walk is, in essence, like riding a horse; sometimes, we will fall off. Every now and then, our fleshly nature will overpower our spiritual man, causing us to act contrary to the way of righteousness.

Paul, himself, dealt with this same challenge as seen in the following words:

> *"I know that nothing good lives in me, that*
> *is, in my sinful nature. For I have the*
> *desire to do what is good, but I cannot*
> *carry it out. For what I do is not the good I*
> *want to do; no, the evil I do not want to do*
> *– this I keep doing. Now if I do what I do*

not want to do, it is no longer I who do it,

but it is sin living in me that does it."

(Romans 7:18-20 NIV).

But Paul never once stopped trying to get it right. We have every reason to believe he understood his position as a child of God, and he was pure at heart. Whenever a setback occurred, or he experienced a failure, he did not attempt to deny it, and he had remorse, all while getting back on the horse to ride again.

However, let me be perfectly clear in explaining, I am not advocating it is okay to indulge in sin, neither am I attempting to downplay our sinful behavior. We must resist the temptation to indulge in whatever it is our flesh loves to indulge in, but just know that sometimes, no matter how hard we fight, the flesh will win. The only thing I am suggesting is when we mess up, if we live in satisfaction, there is a reason to worry then.

Fortunately for us, we cannot disappoint or let God down at any time because the fact He is omniscient means He knows everything there is to know about us, whether past, present, or future. He is well-aware of our shortcomings, long before we commit them and before He calls us into His service, yet He still showers us with mercy. Nevertheless, the Bible reveals there is one unpardonable sin. Jesus declares in the Gospel of Matthew:

"...every sin and blasphemy will be forgiven men, but the blasphemy against the Spirit will not be forgiven. Anyone who speaks a word against the Son of Man will be forgiven, but anyone who speaks against the Holy Spirit will not be forgiven, either in this age or in the age to come." (Matthew 12:31-32 NIV).

Here is what that means: it is the Holy Spirit's job to convict men of their sins and to convict us also to believe. The hearts of those who are not pure will persist in ignoring those convictions and continue living the way they choose, refusing to acknowledge God and surrendering their life to Him. Such a person eventually becomes so cynical that they cannot recognize God's truth and goodness. They reach a point of hardness in which they no longer see, feel, or hear God. They have essentially cursed God's Spirit and counted His convictions as worthless; they have abused, reviled, neglected, ignored, and hardened their heart to the promptings of Holy Spirit permanently – and that, God will not forgive.

So, you see, not all is lost, at least not for every individual. It is not the fact we mess up, which is problematic, and neither does it cause us to smear the church's image. Instead, it is living in denial of our shortcomings and never seeing a need to repent. It is never having remorse for our failures and refusing to agree with God about our sinful condition, thus declining to ask for His forgiveness. It is falling off the horse of righteousness (in a sense) and never attempting to get back on. It is when you knowingly mislead others or when you purposely look the other way on some misdeeds while pointing out others. God's Holy Spirit is doing his part to warn us against doing such things, but are you persistently ignoring the warnings?

If you claim to have morals and Christian values but are reluctant to see the error of your ways and make no effort to change, you are the one who should be concerned with hopelessness. For it is the likes of you that are causing the church's image to be questioned; it is you who are turning people against the idea of gathering in worship with other believers. You are the reason the church is laughed at, ridiculed, or, as I have suggested throughout this writing – *souled-out.*

Conclusion

So, what about you, who finds yourself agreeing with most, if not all I have written? Do you feel this supports your excuse for having nothing to do with being a part of Christ's church (if that is your stance)? Are you further convinced you are better off staying away from the hypocrites and flawed people who make up the various local churches established throughout communities everywhere? If so, you are entirely wrong also! Any change we desire to see in any arena of life begins with us; we must first be the change we long for. Not becoming a part of the solution only makes us part of the problem, which basically falls in line with Christ's teaching. According to Matthew 12:30, he declares:

"Whoever is not with me is against me,
and whoever does not gather with me,
scatters." (NIV).

I understand that for many, Jesus is a controversial figure, and it centers around whether he is the Son of God and the Messiah or not. But regardless of what your view is, make no mistake that his life is one in which we must mimic if we are to find favor with the Father. You can believe he is who he says he is, or you can deny it. However, what you cannot deny is all the Father expects of us is exemplified in the way Jesus lived and conducted himself. Every act of kindness, mercy, compassion, and forgiveness he displayed is to be seen in us. And just as he inner-acted with people, we should, too.

His interactions teach us that no person is an island to themselves; no individual was created to live in isolation. It is in God's plan for each of us to have someone with whom we can lean on to find comfort and support while dealing with the hardships of life. When it comes to people of faith, there is no better environment or stronger support system than being around a community of believers. Therefore, Jesus built the church, and according to Paul's teaching, he gifted the church with,

"...apostles, prophets, evangelists,
pastors, and teachers to prepare God's
people for works of service, so that the
body of Christ may be built up until we all
reach unity in the faith and in the
knowledge of the Son of God and become
mature, attaining to the whole measure of
the fullness of Christ."

(Ephesians 4:11-13 NIV).

You see, I may be going through something you have already gone through, and therefore you can provide the necessary words of comfort and support I need to get through my ordeal. On the flip side, it might be you going through something I have already experienced, in which it then becomes my responsibility to lift you with words of comfort and support. That is how we are to function as a body of believers! It is not our place to sit back in judgment and condemn the church because of the hypocrites or flawed people who make up the congregation. No matter what arena it may be, you will never get away from such people. You work with them, shop with them, dine with them, attend social events with them, live next door to them, even have them in your own family, and better still – you are one of them. Why, then, do you have such a huge problem with people like that, only when it comes to the church?

You need to understand the church will never be perfect as long as it comprises imperfect people. But its success is not contingent upon any of us being flawless; instead, its success depends on our faith and willingness to become a better people by following in the footsteps of Christ. As a people of faith, our goal is to strive toward perfection, realizing that if we stay on course, it will be reached at the end of our journey. So let us

"...press toward the mark for the prize of
the high calling of God in Christ Jesus."
(Philippians 3:14 KJV).

When Jesus declares the gates of hell will not prevail over his church, it is because he knows some will understand this and keep pressing forward. And if only a few get it, that few will no doubt be the universal church. I don't know about you, but at the end of the day, I desire to be in that group!

I want to stand before the Father and hear Him say one day:

> *"Well done, thou good and faithful*
> *servant: thou hast been faithful over a few*
> *things, I will make thee ruler over many*
> *things: enter thou into the joy of thy*
> *Lord." (Matthew 25:21 KJV).*

I always find that verse intriguing because the fact he states, *"...been faithful over a few things..."* suggests the good and faithful servant does not get everything right in life. It's just one who stays loyal to God and His divine will and one who seeks to be a solution to the problems of life rather than be part of them. When you are not with the teachings of Christ or have no desire to follow after his ways, you are against him, and therefore you are part of the problem as well.

So, now that we have had an opportunity to reason

together, I hope when you consider where the fault lies with the church being souled-out, you will realize it lies with all of us. It is not the fault of any particular group of people; instead, it is the fault of each of us collectively. As I have indeed exposed the works of Satan, which is prevalent throughout the membership of local churches, you may have enjoyed what I have done without giving thought to the fact, I exposed you, and I exposed myself as well. We never want to think of ourselves as being Satan's cronies, but often we are, and therefore it's up to us to decide we want that to end now. Let today be the day we all take a stand to improve in some area of our life to help strengthen the church's image. God bless you, and thanks so much for allowing me to have your attention.

About the Author

Kevin Gibbs served in ministry for twenty-five years and has been pastor of two churches for a combined nineteen years. Currently, he serves as Senior Pastor of Zion Missionary Baptist in Jackson, Georgia, where he has been since June 2012.

In 2018, while attending seminary, he took on the task of fulfilling a dream of becoming a published author. He discovered a knack for writing and was often encouraged to pursue it by one of his instructors. His first book "Will Somebody Please Listen" was officially published on October 8, 2019. He tackled the issues surrounding the continuance of injustice in America toward people of color, namely African Americans. He dreams of writing an autobiography detailing how he went from being a standout basketball player in high school to foregoing college and joining the U.S. Air Force to becoming an ordained minister.

Kevin resides in McDonough, GA, along with his wife, Shae, who is also an accomplished author. Together they have a blended family of six children (Ryan, Amber, Jorel, Easha, Keonna, Kevin) and four grandchildren (Joden, Savannah, Heaven, Emoni).

Instagram - kevingibbs_theauthor

Email address - kevingibbstheauthor@gmail.com

Website - www.kevingibbstheauthor.com

Made in the USA
Columbia, SC
21 April 2021